P9-CES-967

To:

_____

From:

_____

Lessons at The Fence Post

Advice for Living, Loving and Working

In loving memory of
George W. Cummings, Sr.,
my Grandfather.

Written and compiled by
Paul D. Cummings

Ballantine Books   •   New York

A Ballantine Book
Published by The Ballantine Publishing Group

www.randomhouse.com/BB/

Library of Congress Catalog Card Number: 99-90171

ISBN 0-345-43287-8

Manufactured in the United States of America

Cover design by Cathy Colbert
Cover photo by Lane Taylor

First Ballantine Books Edition: May 1999

10 9 8 7 6 5 4 3 2 1

Lessons at The Fence Post

A Message from Paul D. Cummings

I was blessed to have a close relationship with my Grandfather, George W. Cummings, Sr., who lived in Conway, Arkansas. My grandfather was a man, rich in principle, who taught me his "Lighthouse" standards for living a high quality life.

In "Lessons at The Fence Post", I detail a collection of the principled lessons which my Grandfather shared with me at a fence post on his farm in Conway. I gained tremendous strength from his wisdom over the years.

It is my hope that you will share these lessons with your friends, family and coworkers. And when someone really wants your advice… do as my Grandfather did… say, "Meet me at the fence post at 5:00 a.m."

As my Grandfather would say if he were still with us… "Ask yourself two questions… What have you learned today and what have you given today?" Answer these questions successfully everyday and you will have a rich life.

A special thanks to my parents, George and Shirley Cummings for their unconditional love and support. You always believed in me and my dream. Thanks Mom and Dad.

I Love You —
Paul D. Cummings

Life is a gift... not a game.

\- George W. Cummings, Sr.
(Grandfather)

Enthusiasm is an inside game

with an outside reflection.

- George W. Cummings, Sr.
(Grandfather)

The dawn of a new day is most beautiful...

when you are awake to see it.

- George W. Cummings, Sr.
(Grandfather)

The only person you need to compete with

or deprive to achieve success

is the man in the mirror.

- George W. Cummings, Sr.
(Grandfather)

Your "Work Ethic" says a lot

about your character.

- George W. Cummings, Sr.
(Grandfather)

You cannot draw water from an empty well...

You cannot give a person what you do not have.

- George W. Cummings, Sr.
(Grandfather)

You must learn to give to others

without expectation of return.

- Paul D. Cummings

Don't worry about those events or circumstances

over which you have no control...

Focus on what you can control.

- George W. Cummings, Sr.
(Grandfather)

Angry words and harsh statements are the winds

of stupidity blowing through your mind and

rolling off your tongue.

- George W. Cummings, Sr.
(Grandfather)

Manage Minutes and Moments

and your life will become Magical.

- Paul D. Cummings

You are one step away in belief

from everything you want in life.

- George W. Cummings, Sr.
(Grandfather)

Always be prepared to hit

the "fat" pitch out of the park.

- George W. Cummings, Sr.
(Grandfather)

We all have a center to our life…

Make sure your center is solid as a rock and

based on principles that do not shift.

- George W. Cummings, Sr.
(Grandfather)

When you gossip it's a strong indication

your own life is not that exciting.

- George W. Cummings, Sr.
(Grandfather)

The road to the top

goes straight through the dump.

- Paul D. Cummings

Don't be a master of all

and a doer of nothing.

- George W. Cummings, Sr.
(Grandfather)

When faced with a disappointment, or a loss, ask

yourself this important question…

What will it matter ten years from now.

- Paul D. Cummings

Nobody ever found a buried treasure without digging for it... Most success is beneath the surface... Dig every day.

- George W. Cummings, Sr.
(Grandfather)

Make sure you have at least 6

good friends before you die.

- George W. Cummings, Sr.
(Grandfather)

When you believe in something with all your

heart... stand up... speak out...

make your voice heard.

- George W. Cummings, Sr.
(Grandfather)

Everybody spends their whole life trying to get there and when they get there... they find out there isn't any there... there. The top of the mountain you are climbing is the bottom of the next peak.

- Paul D. Cummings

The power of a single decision

is immeasurable.

- George W. Cummings, Sr.
(Grandfather)

Son, you cannot get up while looking down...

You must always look upward. You can only soar

with the eagles by looking within.

- George W. Cummings, Sr.
(Grandfather)

In Life by investing money properly… you receive a great return on your investment… The same is true of people. When you invest in yourself properly your value goes up.

- George W. Cummings, Sr.
(Grandfather)

When you make fun of others in a hurtful way...

it's a sure sign of your personal unhappiness.

- George W. Cummings, Sr.
(Grandfather)

If you can't... you must.

- Paul D. Cummings

If you wish to earn more, create a higher

demand for what you provide.

- George W. Cummings, Sr.
(Grandfather)

Remember, if you're in sales… if you serve the customer, the customer will like and trust you.

- George W. Cummings, Sr.
(Grandfather)

We all have a personal gold mine... We carry it

with us every where we go...

Our gold mine is our "Mind."

Tap the resource.

- George W. Cummings, Sr.
(Grandfather)

Remember, life is a marathon not a sprint.

Train yourself to go the distance.

- George W. Cummings, Sr.
(Grandfather)

The fastest horse on earth will never win a race,

or be recognized, or be allowed to fulfill his or

her potential until you put them

on the right track.

- George W. Cummings, Sr.
(Grandfather)

There is no room for prejudice

in life... or business.

- George W. Cummings, Sr.
(Grandfather)

You can't get a positive charge

off a dead battery.

- George W. Cummings, Sr.
(Grandfather)

Praise is the water and nourishment

people need to grow.

- Paul D. Cummings

As long as you have the ability to tell your

parents you love and appreciate them... do it —

this will not always be the case.

- George W. Cummings, Sr.
(Grandfather)

Be an architect, not a laborer... build.

- George W. Cummings, Sr.
(Grandfather)

If you play 3rd base in baseball or life,

be prepared for the line drive.

- George W. Cummings, Sr.
(Grandfather)

You must master the 22 ounces of matter...

that matters... Heart and Head.

- Paul D. Cummings

Every action in life is a matter of personal

choice… Choose to be unique. Choose to be the

best you… you can be.

- George W. Cummings, Sr.
(Grandfather)

43

A man is only poor if he chooses

ignorance as his life's work.

- George W. Cummings, Sr.
(Grandfather)

If you are not good at being you… you will make

a lousy someone else… Be yourself.

- Paul D. Cummings

Life will tempt you every day... Measure all

temptations against your system of value.

- George W. Cummings, Sr.
(Grandfather)

Remember… a kite only rises against the wind.

- Paul D. Cummings

All fires will eventually burn out if you don't consistently tend the fire. Rekindle your personal fire on a daily basis.

- George W. Cummings, Sr.
(Grandfather)

Turn the television off during dinner.

- George W. Cummings, Sr.
(Grandfather)

Every change in life is awkward until you create

a new habit through relentless repetition.

- George W. Cummings, Sr.
(Grandfather)

Make certain the value you bring to others

always exceeds the cost they pay

for your services.

- Paul D. Cummings

51

When you work for an organization you are faced

with a choice... You can put in time or you can

put in everything you have to give.

- George W. Cummings, Sr.
(Grandfather)

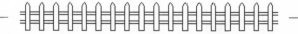

Take 15 minutes off every morning and

afternoon... to relax... breathe... and laugh...

30 minutes for you daily will add years

to your life.

- George W. Cummings, Sr.
(Grandfather)

Listen to music... sing along...

uplift your spirits.

- George W. Cummings, Sr.
(Grandfather)

Balance is necessary for happiness

in all phases of your life.

- George W. Cummings, Sr.
(Grandfather)

The difference between enabled and disabled

employees is their leader or lack thereof.

- Paul D. Cummings

When you ask someone their opinion...

it is a compliment.

- George W. Cummings, Sr.
(Grandfather)

All people operate at their best when they feel needed and appreciated. If you want the best from the people around you... remember this valuable lesson.

- George W. Cummings, Sr.
(Grandfather)

It is never too late to get into the work that is right for you. Don't spend one more second doing that which you don't find stimulating.

- Paul D. Cummings

There is no need to shout about what you are doing for others... Great deeds are easily recognized and always talked about...

- George W. Cummings, Sr.
(Grandfather)

Machines can't change... They become outdated and are replaced with a new improved version... Be thankful you are not a machine... However, through lack of effort you too can become outdated, in need of replacement... like a machine. In today's world you must be willing to change, grow and constantly improve.

- George W. Cummings, Sr.
(Grandfather)

The first key to effective communication is to

know your subject. Knowledge is what to do.

You cannot teach what you do not know.

- George W. Cummings, Sr.
(Grandfather)

As a parent, you lay the foundation for your

children's lives by the habits

you teach and develop.

- George W. Cummings, Sr.
(Grandfather)

Going first class is more a function of purpose

than it is ability to pay.

- George W. Cummings, Sr.
(Grandfather)

Are you hungry son? If the answer is yes... feed

your mind first... then your body...

You will eat less and learn more.

- Paul D. Cummings

Be willing to risk all that you have to gain

all the things you believe in the most.

- George W. Cummings, Sr.
(Grandfather)

Two words you should never forget are

"Thank You."

- George W. Cummings, Sr.
(Grandfather)

Above average, extraordinary people do above average and extraordinary things.

- George W. Cummings, Sr.
(Grandfather)

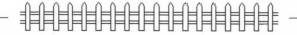

If you are ever granted the privilege of

leadership... be there for your people always.

- George W. Cummings, Sr.
(Grandfather)

You must learn to tie the smallest of Activity

to the largest of Dreams.

- George W. Cummings, Sr.
(Grandfather)

Every person is truly unique...

one of a kind, rare.

- George W. Cummings, Sr.
(Grandfather)

71

Being broke is a temporary situation... wealth

and poverty however are states of mind...

Manage your state daily.

- Paul D. Cummings

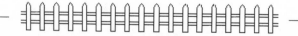

Honesty is your best friend

and dishonesty is your worst enemy.

- George W. Cummings, Sr.
(Grandfather)

It is healthy to be

competitively Angry.

- Paul D. Cummings

People will embrace any idea

backed with conviction.

- George W. Cummings, Sr.
(Grandfather)

Have the vision of an eagle

and the work ethic of a plow horse.

- George W. Cummings, Sr.
(Grandfather)

If you never stoop down...

you will never be able to lift others up.

- George W. Cummings, Sr.
(Grandfather)

Get one hug from somebody

you care about every day.

- George W. Cummings, Sr.
(Grandfather)

Make a list of easy to do things

that you have fun doing.

- George W. Cummings, Sr.
(Grandfather)

If someone looked your name up in the

dictionary… what would the definition be?

- Paul D. Cummings

You can't use your rearview mirror as a guidance

tool... you must look forward with faith.

- George W. Cummings, Sr.
(Grandfather)

Having great wealth is meaningless

unless you use the money for good.

- George W. Cummings, Sr.
(Grandfather)

Mastering relationships is simple...

treat every person you meet as the most

important person in your life.

\- George W. Cummings, Sr.
(Grandfather)

Determination in the face of adversity

is the first step towards courage.

- Paul D. Cummings

When you learn something great... share your

new found knowledge with others.

- George W. Cummings, Sr.
(Grandfather)

Life will never be as frustrating as golf... unless

you live your life in the rough or out of bounds.

- Paul D. Cummings

If you ever lose your enthusiasm

go to a park and watch children at play.

- George W. Cummings, Sr.
(Grandfather)

If you have too many rules for success... you will

always be miserable... Design your life where it

is easy to feel good... and difficult to feel bad.

- George W. Cummings, Sr.
(Grandfather)

All watermelons look good on the outside...

it's what is on the inside that counts.

- George W. Cummings, Sr.
(Grandfather)

Questions unlock the vault

to all human creativity.

- Paul D. Cummings

Your life will never be absent of problems... You must view all problems as an opportunity to learn, to grow... View each obstacle as a stone on which you can sharpen your knife...

- George W. Cummings, Sr.
(Grandfather)

It is better to have skied and fallen…

than never to have skied.

- George W. Cummings, Sr.
(Grandfather)

Pick one skill to develop to a higher level

every 30 days.

- George W. Cummings, Sr.
(Grandfather)

Fear is a positive signal that informs you

something is about to happen

that you are not prepared for.

- Paul D. Cummings

The power of a positive thought! Say this and see what happens: "I am not tired... I am energized."

- George W. Cummings, Sr.
(Grandfather)

Don't question the "Master Plan."

- George W. Cummings, Sr.
(Grandfather)

The farthest distance you'll ever travel is from

your left ear to your right ear.

- Paul D. Cummings

Leadership... the ability to see what no one else sees, to listen when others talk and the ability to be optimistic when others are pessimistic.

- George W. Cummings, Sr.
(Grandfather)

Ask yourself this question… Would I want my

child to repeat my actions of today?

- Paul D. Cummings

It is much easier in life to happily achieve...

than it is for you to achieve so you can be happy.

- George W. Cummings, Sr.
(Grandfather)

You must be an active participant in

some great event at all times.

- George W. Cummings, Sr.
(Grandfather)

Four lessons for living, laughing and loving...

1   *Focus like a laser beam*

2   *Commit to being 1% better daily*

3   *Believe in yourself and others*

4   *Finish what you start*

- Paul D. Cummings

If you truly treasure a friendship...

put more into the relationship than you take out.

- George W. Cummings, Sr.
(Grandfather)

Physical resistance creates muscular growth...

Climb a mountain mentally and

strengthen your mind.

- George W. Cummings, Sr.
(Grandfather)

Keep a journal of your daily activities because if your life is worth living... it is worth recording.

- Paul D. Cummings

Character is doing what is right...

when no one else is watching.

- George W. Cummings, Sr.
(Grandfather)

Learning is sequential...

Sit up... crawl... walk... run... sprint.

- George W. Cummings, Sr.
(Grandfather)

Everyday your actions put another brush stroke

on your canvas of Life. What kind of picture

are you painting today?

- Paul D. Cummings

Whenever you feel like quitting... remember, this is not an original thought... many others felt the same way... many others quit... Do something unique... Press forward with all your strength... Seek to learn something from your experience.

- George W. Cummings, Sr.
(Grandfather)

Never ask anyone to do anything if you don't

intend to measure their performance

and provide them feedback.

- George W. Cummings, Sr.
(Grandfather)

If you have weeds growing in your garden

or your company… you need to take time to work

what you planted.

- George W. Cummings, Sr.
(Grandfather)

A man or woman who smiles with ease possesses

one of God's greatest gifts... peace of mind

- George W. Cummings, Sr.
(Grandfather)

The greatest investment I ever made

was in people.

- George W. Cummings, Sr.
(Grandfather)

When you're angry

always stop and ask yourself this question,

"What will happen if I don't do...

what I am about to do next."

- Paul D. Cummings

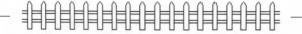

Don't suffer from terminal earwax build up...

Listen.

- George W. Cummings, Sr.
(Grandfather)

Keep your Game Face on.

Operate with Focused and Channeled Energy.

- Paul D. Cummings

Before you hire someone…

find out how he or she defines success.

- George W. Cummings, Sr.
(Grandfather)

You must learn to look at life

through childlike eyes.

- George W. Cummings, Sr.
(Grandfather)

You can not hope yourself to greatness.

\- George W. Cummings, Sr.
(Grandfather)

Arguments are like accidents… They can be

spotted from a distance and avoided easily.

- George W. Cummings, Sr.
(Grandfather)

Do what you must do, when you must do it...

whether you like it or not.

- George W. Cummings, Sr.
(Grandfather)

The ability to imagine… to remain curious…

creates a fountain of new ideas

upon which to act.

\- Paul D. Cummings

You must let go… to grow.

- George W. Cummings, Sr.
(Grandfather)

Discipline is not the enemy

of enthusiasm.

- George W. Cummings, Sr.
(Grandfather)

Never settle for Second Place

when First is available.

- George W. Cummings, Sr.
(Grandfather)

Be Rigid in Principle...

Flexible in Approach.

- George W. Cummings, Sr.
(Grandfather)

Learn to pass positives down,

and negatives up.

- George W. Cummings, Sr.
(Grandfather)

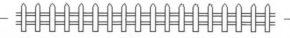

You must take Personal Responsibility for

Individual Daily Effort.

- George W. Cummings, Sr.
(Grandfather)

Do the thing you fear and the

death of fear is certain.

- Paul D. Cummings

Self-Discipline is the Master Key

to all riches.

- George W. Cummings, Sr.
(Grandfather)

There is gold at the end of effort.

- George W. Cummings, Sr.
(Grandfather)

When in doubt…

sling effort at it!

- George W. Cummings, Sr.
(Grandfather)

There should never be anything anyone can ever

say or do that would convince you that you are

anything less than 100% the best

at what you do.

- Paul D. Cummings

As children... we all drew pictures, painted with

finger paint, chalk... We were an artist... As

adults we stop drawing and start working...

Stop right now... You are an artist.

What have you drawn lately?

- George W. Cummings, Sr.
(Grandfather)

When you wake up in the

morning... check for a pulse . . .

when you find one... go nuts.

- George W. Cummings, Sr.
(Grandfather)

Laugh at yourself...

You really are funny.

- George W. Cummings, Sr.
(Grandfather)

Set yourself on fire with enthusiasm.

- Paul D. Cummings

If you Preach It and Teach It long enough…

they will Get It.

- George W. Cummings, Sr.
(Grandfather)

You will never seriously desire that which you do not have the ability to achieve.

- George W. Cummings, Sr.
(Grandfather)

When you see someone who cares for others...

you see someone who also cares for themself.

- George W. Cummings, Sr.
(Grandfather)

I trust myself more than I do the government

to take care of my future...

That's why I save my money.

- George W. Cummings, Sr.
(Grandfather)

141

You need not ever sacrifice your honesty,

integrity or character to make a dollar.

- George W. Cummings, Sr.
(Grandfather)

Don't ever underestimate the power of humility.

- Paul D. Cummings

Never reject an idea you know little about...

Become curious... Use your skepticism as the first

step towards the acquisition of New Knowledge.

- George W. Cummings, Sr.
(Grandfather)

If your bank account is larger than your bank of

friends... change your focus

- George W. Cummings, Sr.
(Grandfather)

Anything you do that blemishes your integrity is more than wrong... it is shameful.

- George W. Cummings, Sr.
(Grandfather)

When you have a gift… use it…

When you have a chance… take it…

When you need to risk… risk it.

- George W. Cummings, Sr.
(Grandfather)

147

You must be like a rubberband...

you're most useful when you stretch.

- George W. Cummings, Sr.
(Grandfather)

The difference between Passion and Passionate

lies in your ability to share that which

you feel with others.

- George W. Cummings, Sr.
(Grandfather)

You will only treat others as kindly

as you treat yourself.

- Paul D. Cummings

Sometimes the most complicated task in life...

is to keep things simple.

- George W. Cummings, Sr.
(Grandfather)

Success is the big oak tree you climbed with no fear during your youth... that today you wouldn't climb because of your age.

- George W. Cummings, Sr.
(Grandfather)

Everything in life that matters the most

can't be purchased.

- Paul D. Cummings

Advertise on the screen of your mind those things

in life you passionately wish to achieve.

- George W. Cummings, Sr.
(Grandfather)

You will not die from hard work...

you will pass out first...

Then you can rest.

- George W. Cummings, Sr.
(Grandfather)

Worry is like a rocking chair... you expend a lot

of energy... and never get anywhere.

- George W. Cummings, Sr.
(Grandfather)

Take adversity... turn it into

challenge and create opportunity.

- George W. Cummings, Sr.
(Grandfather)

157

Do something great for someone everyday

and don't get caught.

- George W. Cummings, Sr.
(Grandfather)

Remember to enjoy the moment...

We are only here for a flicker in the span of time.

- George W. Cummings, Sr.
(Grandfather)

When you have to take a dose of

medicine... take it.

- George W. Cummings, Sr.
(Grandfather)

Problems are opportunity

disguised as obstacles.

- Paul D. Cummings

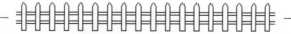

Treat each day as an opportunity you have been

given to truly make a difference in the life of

each person you meet.

- George W. Cummings, Sr.
(Grandfather)

I never was interested in being a spectator... I wanted to play with one thought... to win.

- George W. Cummings, Sr.
(Grandfather)

When you do something wrong... you are the

first one to know.

- Paul D. Cummings

You can't get lost

on a straight track.

- George W. Cummings, Sr.
(Grandfather)

Don't be like the hunter who stands at the side of the woods and shoots his gun and then shouts, "I hope that runs into something." Have a target in mind.

- George W. Cummings, Sr.
(Grandfather)

Life is not dull and boring unless you approach

life in a dull, boring fashion.

- George W. Cummings, Sr.
(Grandfather)

Sometimes it's okay to say shut up...

if you're talking to yourself.

- George W. Cummings, Sr.
(Grandfather)

At the end of your day... ask this simple question... Are you proud of what you did today?

- Paul D. Cummings

Always teach employees what you want them to

do before you ask them to accomplish the task.

- George W. Cummings, Sr.
(Grandfather)

Light the way for others by

being a "Shining" example of "Right" Living.

- George W. Cummings, Sr.
(Grandfather)

Sometimes you need to catch up to catch on...

Educate yourself.

- Paul D. Cummings

You are here for a reason… You must trust yourself and believe in your self-worth if you desire success.

- George W. Cummings, Sr.
(Grandfather)

Don't wait till the middle of winter

to buy a coat.

- George W. Cummings, Sr.
(Grandfather)

Criticism is only delivered by a person

who can't offer constructive guidance.

- George W. Cummings, Sr.
(Grandfather)

Your love of God, family and country

should be boundaryless.

- George W. Cummings, Sr.
(Grandfather)

Develop a personal Code of Conduct

and Live by it.

- George W. Cummings, Sr.
(Grandfather)

Customers see value only in that which is

presented with conviction and enthusiasm.

- Paul D. Cummings

Life may not always seem fair but you can

always be fair in the way you conduct your life.

- George W. Cummings, Sr.
(Grandfather)

If you are going to wear a suit...

shine your shoes.

- George W. Cummings, Sr.
(Grandfather)

Most of what you worry about will never happen.

- George W. Cummings, Sr.
(Grandfather)

All external reward comes about

as a result of internal effort.

- Paul D. Cummings

Limits are self imposed barriers

we place on ourself.

- George W. Cummings, Sr.
(Grandfather)

To understand another's point of view is sure

proof of your open mind.

- George W. Cummings, Sr.
(Grandfather)

Never tell your children, "I already know that."

You will extinguish their eagerness to share

their feelings with you.

- Paul D. Cummings

Teach your children to save money...

Everyone else will teach them how to spend it.

- George W. Cummings, Sr.
(Grandfather)

Every person you meet in life

has a flashing sign on their chest...

It says, "Make Me Feel Special."

- George W. Cummings, Sr.
(Grandfather)

The old saying, "You can lead a horse to water...

but you can't make him drink..." is a

misperception... If you SALT the horse's OATS

and make him thirsty he will drink all day...

- George W. Cummings, Sr.
(Grandfather)

If you don't "Belly Laugh" at least 3 times a

day… you are cutting your life short

by personal choice.

- George W. Cummings, Sr.
(Grandfather)

Some people treat problems like hemorrhoids...

They sit on them and hope they will clear up.

- George W. Cummings, Sr.
(Grandfather)

If you don't know your business… someone else

will own your business.

- George W. Cummings, Sr.
(Grandfather)

Use nickel words to describe million dollar ideas.

- George W. Cummings, Sr.
(Grandfather)

Master Time... And you win.

Do What's Important Now.

- George W. Cummings, Sr.
(Grandfather)

The Ultimate Standard of Excellence:

Consistency

Every Day...

Every Time...

Without Fail...

No Exceptions.

- Paul D. Cummings

Never be afraid to fail... Mistakes provide you

with opportunities for continual growth.

- George W. Cummings, Sr.
(Grandfather)

Patience allows you to master events that other

people view as overwhelming.

- George W. Cummings, Sr.
(Grandfather)

Defend your opinions, but never operate under

the illusion that your opinions

are always correct.

- George W. Cummings, Sr.
(Grandfather)

When you make a choice to exclude yourself from

the struggles of Life... you have also chosen to

exclude yourself from the true riches

Life has to offer.

- George W. Cummings, Sr.
(Grandfather)

When you are in error... admit your mistake...

It's okay to say "I was wrong."

- George W. Cummings, Sr.
(Grandfather)

Don't try to be too smart…

When you over analyze your intellect

you will paralyze your creativity.

- George W. Cummings, Sr.
(Grandfather)

When choosing companions for Life...

be sure to include patience, wisdom and health.

- George W. Cummings, Sr.
(Grandfather)

Become solution oriented... not worry oriented

and you will find pleasure where others

find pain and discomfort.

- George W. Cummings, Sr.
(Grandfather)

He who toots his own horn...

plays in a one man band forever.

- George W. Cummings, Sr.
(Grandfather)

If you would like to submit a family wisdom or unique personal expression for printing in future Fence Post volumes, please write to me at the address below:

Paul D. Cummings
3203 Ringgold Road
Chattanooga, Tennessee 37412

EMAIL: tsi1@chatt.mindspring.com

Please include your name, address and phone number.